AF375225

"Thank you, Lord, for the opportunity to use what

you have given me to bring you glory.

I dedicate this to my own multiple arrows, I can't wait to read this to you.

And to all the 3800+ children I have hugged and ministered to.

Thank you to Bishop Gary and Pastor Debbie for your love and support,

Tori Kate for being so patient, so funny and for creating

such beautiful illustrations,

Ashley and Garrett for your love and generosity,

Apostle Debra, Rev Faithful for your encouragement and prayers,

Tammi Curley, Grace Kelly, and Erica Lucas for your wonderful support,

Liz and Amanda, you ladies are rockstars!"

- Shiloh Moyo

"Thank you to Jon, for your ongoing support through the making of this

book; and to my little monkeys, you're simply the best."

-Tori Kate

Scan here for a special audio read-along with Shiloh!

The Floating Zoo: A humorous story about Noah's Ark

Copyright © 2023 by Shiloh Moyo. All rights reserved.

Illustrations © 2023 by Tori Kate Heavenor

ISBN: 979 8 9884813 0 0

First Edition: 2023
Published by Shiloh Moyo
Printed in United States

This story was inspired by the original Biblical Account of Noah's Ark in Genesis 6-9 NKJV.
Any similarity to actual persons, living or dead, or actual events is purely coincidental and unintentional.
The characters and events portrayed in this book are fictional. Any resemblance to any real individuals or events is purely coincidental.

For permissions, please contact: Shiloh Moyo, A325-5568, 200 N Vineyard Blvd. Honolulu, HI 96817, USA

This story is taken from the story of Noah's Ark in the Bible. While this version has been written to show some of the emotions Noah may have felt, our intention is not to change the integrity of the original story from The Bible. We wanted to highlight an aspect of it without compromising the integrity of the Scripture.

Cover design by Tori Heavenor and Shiloh Moyo

THE FLOATING ZOO

Written by Shiloh Moyo

Illustrated by Tori Kate

Right after Noah's 500th birthday,
all seemed to be going as planned.

But then God came to Noah with a command
and Noah, having no clue what
was about to happen, said,

"Yes Lord, I can!"

"Noah, Noah, everyone has been bad.
Only you have found favor in all the land.

I am sending lots of rain to cover the earth.
Get to work, Noah! This is what I've planned."

Oh, this is a disaster! What will we do?
Where will we hide this Ginormous Floating Zoo?

But no matter what the nosy neighbors
thought when they came to inspect,

Noah had to obey God,
and not let rejection make him upset.

"There goes the Ark Weirdo with a beard-o!"
the neighbors all sneered.

"What if we lose all our friends, Dad?"
Noah's sons yelled, telling Noah what they feared.

Let all the
animals know,
that they will go
two by two.

All aboard for a
long adventure
on the Floating Zoo!

WAIT!
Won't it be chaotic with all these animals
on this thing called a Floating Zoo?
This has never happened before!
What on earth should Noah do?

If all the animals were coming,
there needed to be some rules:

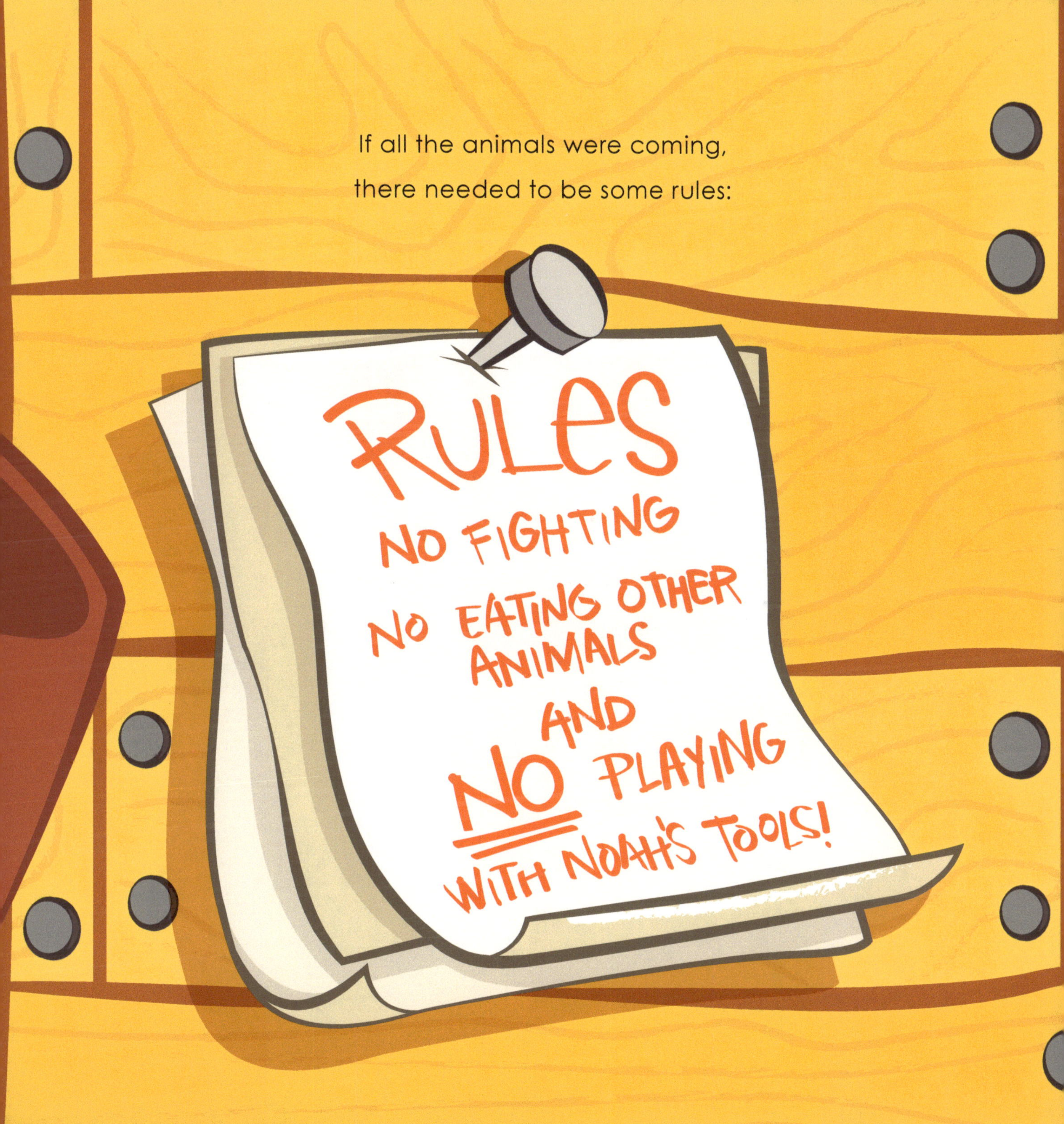

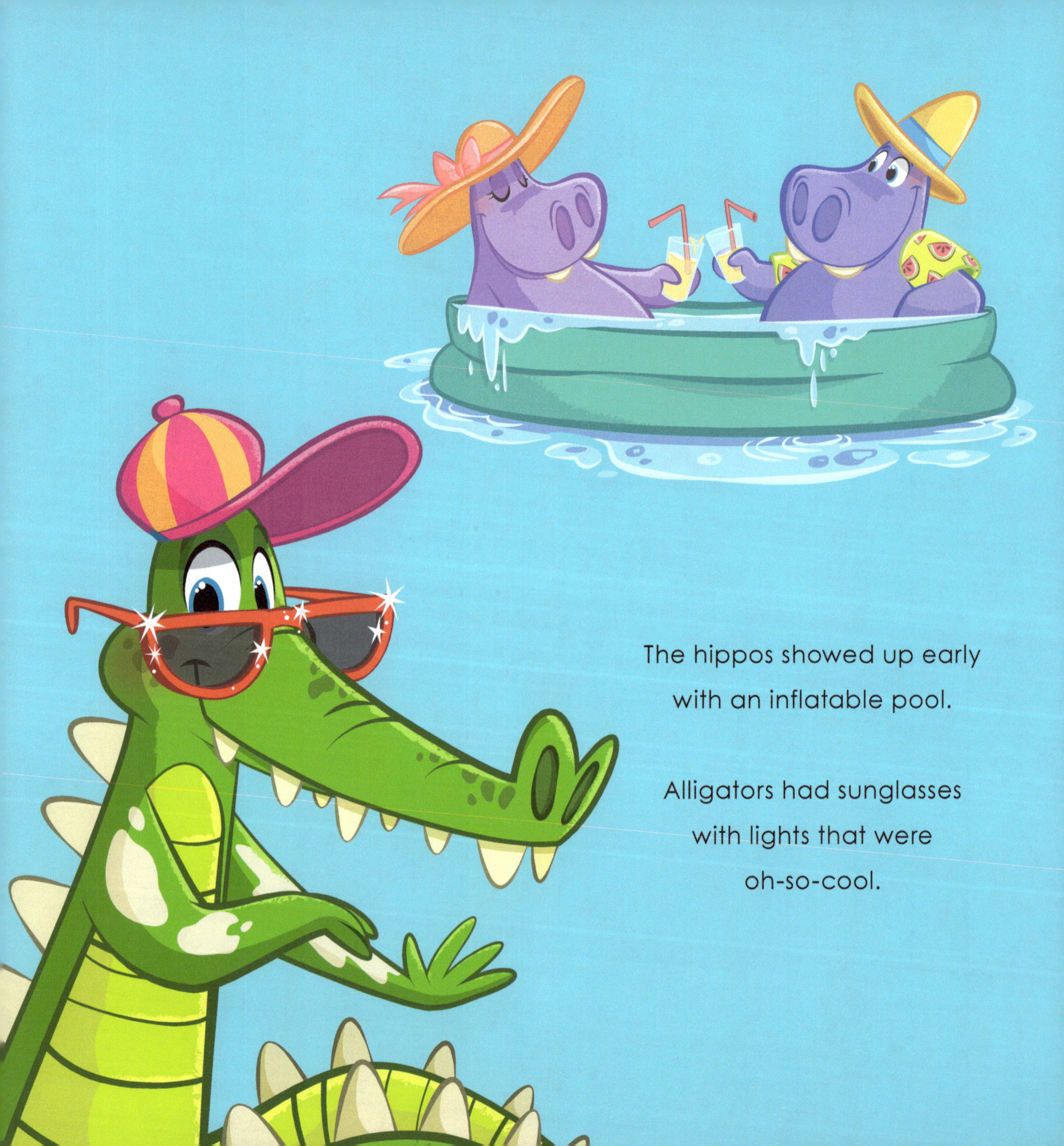

The hippos showed up early
with an inflatable pool.

Alligators had sunglasses
with lights that were
oh-so-cool.

The puffins, and flamingoes caused a commotion,
"Oh, we hope we didn't forget anything?!"
They screeched with emotion.

Raccoons sprang into action,
being so clever and quick.
Guiding lazy llamas and gorillas,
with a kick.

The termites appeared,
ready to munch and chew.
A reminder was needed,
so here's what they knew:

"Hey little termites, the wood's not
your snack. Find something else to
nibble, let's keep the wood intact!"

The giraffes wrote a letter of complaint,
requesting a room far away from the lions.

Sadly, carnivores were invited,
and the poor zebras just wanted to faint!

Noah had a hard time sending the cows and deer to bed because they hid from the hungry lions under Noah's bed.

Fearing the lions would snack on them,
even though the lions had just been fed,

Noah had to assure the herbivores,
to stop being paranoid, and just

GO TO BED!

"This is only day two!" tired Noah sighed.

"Does God have **ANY** idea what I am going through?"

And as if things just couldn't get worse the whales, horses, and piggies caught the flu!

Pigeons pooping everywhere
and the camels shedding their hair.

Mischievous monkeys getting up to no good.
Nothing was working out the way it should!

Fun-loving foxes won't go to bed.

Stinky skunks play games instead.

Tootin' turkeys dream of outdoors.

Panda poops all over the floors.

What are we going to do?

Dreadful, disastrous animal behavior on the Floating Zoo!

Every animal driving
Noah completely
NUTs!

Noah yells,

Parrot problems and penguin parties.

Apes trying to escape.

What in the world are we going to do?

Everybody blames poor Noah

for the idea of the Floating Zoo.

Emotional elephants can't find their stuff,

"That's it!"

Noah yells,

"I have had enough!"

As the rain continued to fall, and winds blow,
Noah gathered all the animals,
as the Ark rocked to and fro.

"Everybody behave!
 Let me tell you a story," he said.
And suddenly the animals stopped fussing
and listened instead.
They were all amazed as Noah described
God's amazing, incredible plan.

They listened in awe as Noah described
the wondrous plan God had devised.
He told them about the sins, the Ark and the rain,
And how the neighbors thought he was totally insane.

Noah sent out a dove that found a place to land,
And it returned to the Ark with an olive leaf
as God had planned.
The rain finally stopped, and the flood water receded.
Finally, Noah knew the mission was completed.

And then in a beautiful sky a rainbow appeared—
A sign of God's promise that there was nothing to be feared.

Noah and his wife sat together as they soaked up the sun,
Thankful and relieved for everything God had done.

THE END

Shiloh Moyo

Shiloh is a hive of creativity who loves children, cake and Capri, Italy. She is a Pastor and has ministered to and taught more than 3800 children. She is also an artist, musician and is always up for a good laugh. Shiloh is originally from a little country, called Zimbabwe, in Southern Africa, where there are plenty of adventures and wild animals. This is her first children's book, but certainly not the last!

Tori Kate

Tori has loved drawing and creating colorful characters since she was a young kid. She always dreamed of becoming an artist and creating children's storybooks! Besides drawing, Tori loves reading, baking sweet treats, and spending time outdoors with her husband and two kids in Vancouver, Canada.